My MyTe Musings

One Insight ...
One Choice ...
One Action ...
At a Time ™

k d MarLee

www.B-MyTe.com

To give somebody your time
is the biggest gift you can give.
~ Franka Potente

You are valuable.
Give yourself the gift of time to
pause, reflect and refresh.

ISBN: 978-0-9837821-6-2

How to Use This Book in Your Journey to B-MyTe

1. This book is meant to be a journal of your thoughts and insights as you experience your daily life and any changes that may be happening to you or around you.

2. You can fill in the book from front to back, or flip through the pages to find a quote that resonates with you. Jot down your thoughts and any insights on that page. You might want to date your entries.

3. As you write in the book, note which quotes were the most inspirational for you at that time. How did the quotes help you?

4. Keep the journal handy and periodically review the quotes again. You will find that different quotes will resonate with you differently as you journey through your life.

The hardest thing to find in life is balance—especially the more success you have, the more you look to the other side of the gate. What do I need to stay grounded, in touch, in love, connected, emotionally balanced? Look within yourself.

~ Celine Dion

Getting started ...

Breathe deeply. Hold for a few seconds. Prepare to muse and write on the following pages. And let it go!

Stretch.

Take a moment to:

> Think of something to make you smile or laugh.
>
> Find someone or something to be thankful for.
>
> Reflect on the beauty around you.
>
> Ponder who or what is important to you.

Take charge of your own life.

Choose respect toward yourself and others.

At the end of the day, reflect: How MyTe was I today?

Motivation is what gets you started.
Habit is what keeps you going.
~ Jim Rohn

_____

_____

_____

_____

_____

_____

_____

_____

_____

_____

_____

_____

_____

_____

_____

_____

_____

_____

Money cannot buy peace of mind. It cannot heal ruptured relationships, or build meaning into a life that has none.

~ Richard M. DeVos

Persist—don't take no for an answer. If you're happy to sit at your desk and not take any risk, you'll be sitting at your desk for the next twenty years.

~ David Rubenstein

No person, no place, and no thing has any power over us, for 'we' are the only thinkers in our mind. When we create peace and harmony and balance in our minds, we will find it in our lives.

~ Louise L. Hay

_____

_____

_____

_____

_____

_____

_____

_____

_____

_____

_____

_____

_____

_____

_____

_____

You have to work hard to get your thinking clean to make it simple. But it's worth it in the end because once you get there, you can move mountains.
~ Steve Jobs

The greatest discovery of all time is that
a person can change his future by merely
changing his attitude.
            ~ Oprah Winfrey

_____

_____

_____

_____

_____

_____

_____

_____

_____

_____

_____

_____

_____

_____

_____

_____

_____

_____

This company looks cheap, that company looks cheap, but the overall economy could completely screw it up. The key is to wait. Sometimes the hardest thing to do is to do nothing.

~ David Tepper

The key to success is to focus our conscious mind on things we desire not things we fear.
~ Brian Tracy

A well-developed sense of humor is the pole
that adds balance to your steps as you walk
the tightrope of life.
~ William Arthur Ward

_____

_____

_____

_____

_____

_____

_____

_____

_____

_____

_____

_____

_____

_____

_____

_____

_____

Life is like an ice-cream cone, you have to
lick it one day at a time.
~ Charles M. Schulz

I think anything is possible if you have the mindset and the will and desire to do it and put the time in.

~ Roger Clemens

Take time to be kind and to say thank you.
~ Zig Ziglar

Control and surrender have to be kept in balance. That's what surfers do—take control of the situation, then be carried, then take control.

~ Brian Eno

_____

_____

_____

_____

_____

_____

_____

_____

_____

_____

_____

_____

_____

_____

_____

_____

_____

_____

But if you can create an honorable livelihood, where you take your skills and use them and you earn a living from it, it gives you a sense of freedom and allows you to balance your life the way you want.

~ Anita Roddick

Successful entrepreneurs find the balance between listening to their inner voice and staying persistent in driving for success— because sometimes success is waiting right across from the transitional bump that's disguised as failure.

~ Naveen Jain

It is not enough to be busy; so are the ants. The
question is: What are we busy about?
~ Henry David Thoreau

Time goes on. So whatever you're going to do,
do it. Do it now. Don't wait.
~ Robert De Niro

You can't start with imbalance and end with peace, be that in your own body, in an ecosystem or between a government and its people. What we need to strive for is not perfection, but balance.

~ Ani DiFranco

Your body hears everything your mind says.
~ Naomi Judd

Today I choose life. Every morning when I wake up I can choose joy, happiness, negativity, pain ... To feel the freedom that comes from being able to continue to make mistakes and choices—today I choose to feel life, not to deny my humanity but embrace it.

~ Viktor E. Frankl

You can't build a great building on a weak foundation. You must have a solid foundation if you're going to have a strong superstructure.
~ Gordon B. Hinckley

_____

_____

_____

_____

_____

_____

_____

_____

_____

_____

_____

_____

_____

_____

_____

_____

_____

_____

When you have confidence, you can have a lot of fun. And when you have fun, you can do amazing things.
~ Joe Namath

A business has to be involving, it has to
be fun, and it has to exercise your creative
instincts.

~ Richard Branson

We are driven by five genetic needs: survival,
love and belonging, power, freedom, and fun.
~ William Glasser

I believe that the greatest gift you can give
your family and the world is a healthy you.
~ Joyce Meyer

_____

_____

_____

_____

_____

_____

_____

_____

_____

_____

_____

_____

_____

_____

_____

_____

Hearty laughter is a good way to jog internally
without having to go outdoors.
~ Norman Cousins

Cheerfulness is the best promoter of health
and is as friendly to the mind as to the body.
~ Joseph Addison

Between stimulus and response there is a space. In that space is our power to choose our response. In our response lies our growth and our freedom.
~ Viktor E. Frankl

Laughter is important, not only because it makes us happy, it also has actual health benefits. And that's because laughter completely engages the body and releases the mind. It connects us to others, and that in itself has a healing effect.

~ Marlo Thomas

An investment in knowledge pays the best interest.

~ Benjamin Franklin

The foundation stones for a balanced success are honesty, character, integrity, faith, love and loyalty.

~ Zig Ziglar

Your vision becomes clear when you look inside your heart. Who looks outside, dreams. Who looks inside, awakens.

~ Carl Gustav Jung

We are what we repeatedly do. Excellence, then, is not an act, but a habit.
~ Aristotle

_____

_____

_____

_____

_____

_____

_____

_____

_____

_____

_____

_____

_____

_____

_____

_____

_____

Moral authority comes from following universal and timeless principles like honesty, integrity, treating people with respect.
~ Stephen Covey

Every great dream begins with a dreamer. Always remember you have within you the strength, the patience and the passion to reach for the stars, to change the world.

~ Harriet Tubman

Action and reaction, ebb and flow, trial and error, change—this is the rhythm of living. Out of our over-confidence, fear; out of our fear, clearer vision, fresh hope. And out of hope, progress.

~ Bruce Barton

The main problem with this great obsession for saving time is very simple: you can't save time. You can only spend it. But you can spend it wisely or foolishly.

~ Benjamin Hoff

Until you value yourself, you won't value your
time. Until you value your time, you will not do
anything with it.

~ M. Scott Peck

There's a lot of people in this world who spend so much time watching their health that they haven't the time to enjoy it.
~ Josh Billings

Know what you own, and know why you own it.

~ Peter Lynch

Time is too slow for those who wait, too swift
for those who fear, too long for those who
grieve, too short for those who rejoice, but for
those who love, time is eternity.
~ Henry Van Dyke

You cannot control what happens to you, but you can control your attitude toward what happens to you, and in that, you will be mastering change rather than allowing it to master you.

~ Brian Tracy

Learn to enjoy every minute of your life. Be happy now. Don't wait for something outside of yourself to make you happy in the future. Think how really precious is the time you have to spend, whether it's at work or with your family. Every minute should be enjoyed and savored.
~ Earl Nightingale

_____

_____

_____

_____

_____

_____

_____

_____

_____

_____

_____

_____

_____

_____

_____

Respect is one of life's greatest treasures. I mean,
what does it all add up to if you don't have that?
~ Marilyn Monroe

Once you appreciate one of your blessings, one of your senses, your sense of hearing, then you begin to respect the sense of seeing and touching and tasting, you learn to respect all the senses.
~ Maya Angelou

When you practice gratefulness, there is a
sense of respect toward others.
~ Dalai Lama

Have the courage to say no. Have the courage to face the truth. Do the right thing because it is right. These are the magic keys to living your life with integrity.

~ W. Clement Stone

_____

_____

_____

_____

_____

_____

_____

_____

_____

_____

_____

_____

_____

_____

_____

_____

_____

_____

Rest is not idleness, and to lie sometimes on the grass under trees on a summer's day, listening to the murmur of the water, or watching the clouds float across the sky, is by no means a waste of time.

~ John Lubbock

The foundation of success in life is good health: that is the substratum fortune; it is also the basis of happiness. A person cannot accumulate a fortune very well when he is sick.

~ P. T. Barnum

One of the most sincere forms of respect is
actually listening to what another has to say.
~ Bryant H. McGill

Emancipate yourselves from mental slavery,
none but ourselves can free our minds!
~ Bob Marley

Respect is one of the greatest expressions of love.

~ Miguel Angel Ruiz

We ourselves feel that what we are doing is just a drop in the ocean. But the ocean would be less because of that missing drop.
~ Mother Teresa

Ethics is knowing the difference between what you have a right to do and what is right to do.

~ Potter Stewart

Happiness is not a matter of intensity but of balance, order, rhythm and harmony.
~ Thomas Merton

Ethics is a code of values which guide our choices and actions and determine the purpose and course of our lives.

~ Ayn Rand

Two things fill my mind with ever-increasing
wonder and awe: the starry heavens above me
and the moral law within me.

~ Immanuel Kant

_____

_____

_____

_____

_____

_____

_____

_____

_____

_____

_____

_____

_____

_____

_____

_____

_____

_____

The first step in the evolution of ethics is a sense
of solidarity with other human beings.
~ Albert Schweitzer

_____

_____

_____

_____

_____

_____

_____

_____

_____

_____

_____

_____

_____

_____

_____

_____

_____

Just as your car runs more smoothly and requires less energy to go faster and farther when the wheels are in perfect alignment, you perform better when your thoughts, feelings, emotions, goals, and values are in balance.

~ Brian Tracy

For to be free is not merely to cast off one's chains, but to live in a way that respects and enhances the freedom of others.

~ Nelson Mandela

They always say time changes things, but
you actually have to change them yourself.
~ Andy Warhol

_____

_____

_____

_____

_____

_____

_____

_____

_____

_____

_____

_____

_____

_____

_____

_____

_____

Nothing is less important than which fork
you use. Etiquette is the science of living. It
embraces everything. It is ethics. It is honor.
~ Emily Post

Watch your thoughts, for they become words.
Watch your words, for they become actions.
Watch your actions, for they become habits.
Watch your habits, for they become character.
Watch your character, for it becomes your destiny.
~ Ralph Waldo Emerson

But if you can create an honorable livelihood, where you take your skills and use them and you earn a living from it, it gives you a sense of freedom and allows you to balance your life the way you want.

~ Anita Roddick

Let your life lightly dance on the edges of
Time like dew on the tip of a leaf.
~ Rabindranath Tagore

You will never find time for anything. If you want time, you must make it.
~ Charles Buxton

As long as we are persistent in our pursuit of our deepest destiny, we will continue to grow. We cannot choose the day or time when we will fully bloom. It happens in its own time.
~ Denis Waitley

Responsibility is the price of freedom.
~ Elbert Hubbard

Time isn't precious at all, because it is an illusion. What you perceive as precious is not time but the one point that is out of time: the Now. That is precious indeed. The more you are focused on time—past and future—the more you miss the Now, the most precious thing there is.

~ Eckhart Tolle

By taking the time to stop and appreciate who you
are and what you've achieved—and perhaps learned
through a few mistakes, stumbles and losses—you
actually can enhance everything about you. Self-
acknowledgement and appreciation are what give you
the insights and awareness to move forward toward
higher goals and accomplishments.

~ Jack Canfield

_____

_____

_____

_____

_____

_____

_____

_____

_____

_____

_____

_____

_____

_____

Money is only a tool. It will take you
wherever you wish, but it will not replace you as
the driver.

~ Ayn Rand

More than anything else, what differentiates people who live up to their potential from those who don't is a willingness to look at themselves and others objectively.

~ Ray Dalio

The older I get, the more I see a straight path where I want to go. If you're going to hunt elephants, don't get off the trail for a rabbit.

~ T. Boone Pickens

The first wealth is health.
~ Ralph Waldo Emerson

Innovation distinguishes between a leader and a follower.

~ Steve Jobs

_____
_____
_____
_____
_____
_____
_____
_____
_____
_____
_____
_____
_____
_____
_____
_____
_____
_____

It is not the beauty of a building you should look at; it's the construction of the foundation that will stand the test of time.

~ David Allan Coe

The foundation stones for a balanced success are honesty, character, integrity, faith, love and loyalty.

~ Zig Ziglar

Time = Life, therefore, waste your time and waste your life, or master your time and master your life.

~ Alan Lakein

I am free because I know that I alone am morally responsible for everything I do. I am free, no matter what rules surround me. If I find them tolerable, I tolerate them; if I find them too obnoxious, I break them. I am free because I know that I alone am morally responsible for everything I do.

~ Robert A. Heinlein

What lies behind you and what lies in front of you, pales in comparison to what lies inside of you.

~ Ralph Waldo Emerson

Need a Reminder?

Use the **MyTe Handy Formula**
to remind yourself how to
find more balance as you discover:

One Insight ...
One Choice ...
One Action ...
At a Time™

Foundation + Focus + Feel+ Flow + Fun =
Freedom™

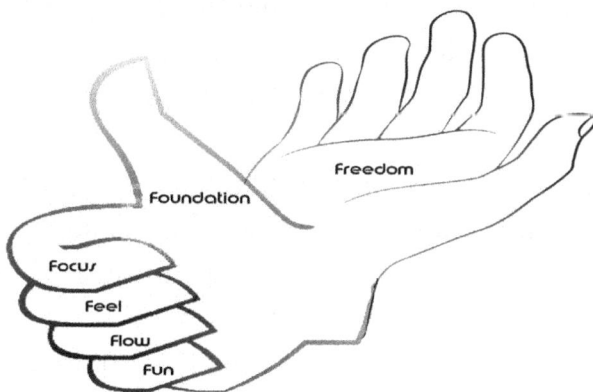

Your hand and your musings combine
to help you B-MyTe.

www.B-MyTe.com

Who We Are

k d MarLee is the pseudonym of two authors writing as one. The goal of their collaboration is to produce work that is inspired, creative, and joyful. k Mar's journey has led her to focus on living with integrity and enjoying her work. Her passion for ethics and aptitude for numbers gives her a unique perspective on living a balanced life. d Lee has always looked on the bright side of life, using her positive disposition to stay open to life's experiences. Her days are spent balancing creative inspiration with the practical side of passion.

Drawing from k Mar's background in philosophy, and d Lee's background in finance, they have built a thriving bookkeeping firm. For over 11 years, they have assisted small business owners with the tracking and analysis of their money and time. As they began to write together, k Mar and d Lee mixed their experiences to achieve a blend of dynamic energy. As writers, they have shown the knowledge and wisdom they have learned, both as entrepreneurs and throughout their lives.

As k d MarLee, they have combined their writing voices and been published in chapters of collaboration books such as the series *Wake Up, Live the Life you Love*, and self-published books under their own brand Catalyst for Creative Living at www.catalystfor-creativeliving.com. Most recently, they have pioneered a proven formula for change called the *MyTe Handy Formula*. They are presenting this formula in their show on VoiceAmerica Empowerment Channel called *B-MyTe: Balancing your Money and your Time*.

www.B-MyTe.com

www.ingramcontent.com/pod-product-compliance
Lightning Source LLC
Chambersburg PA
CBHW070807050426
42452CB00011B/1928